An Nasihah

Islamic Curriculum

المنهج الاسلامي للأطفال

Workbook 6

Girls

When Allāh wishes good for someone, He bestows upon him the understanding of dīn. From Ṣaḥīḥ al-Bukhārī.

- Fiqh
- Aḥādīth
- Sīrah
- Tārīkh
- `Aqā'id
- Akhlāq
- Ādāb

An Nasihah Publications

4th edition June 2019

British Library Cataloguing in Publication Data. A catalogue record for this book is available from the British Library.

Every effort has been made to ensure the correctness of the content. The publishers will gladly receive information enabling them to rectify any error or omission in subsequent editions.

An Nasihah Publications Ltd.
114 Harborough Road
Leicester LE2 4LD
United Kingdom
www.an-nasihah.com
admin@an-nasihah.com

Distributor in the UK
Azhar Academy, London
020 8911 9797
www.azharacademy.com
sales@azharacademy.com

Distributor in Canada
Mawlana Zakariyya Desai
647-781-7313
nasihahcanada@gmail.com

Distributors in Australia
Melbourne, Victoria
Mufti Zeeyad Ravat
0499 559 199
zravat@hotmail.com

Perth, Western Australia
Shaykh Burhaan Mehtar
0452 217 866
iqraacademyperth@gmail.com

Printed by Imak Offset in Turkey

Name: ______________________

Class: ______________________

اَلْحَمْدُ لِلّٰهِ رَبِّ الْعَالَمِيْنَ
وَالصَّلَاةُ وَالسَّلَامُ عَلٰى نَبِيِّنَا مُحَمَّدٍ
وَعَلٰى اٰلِهٖ وَصَحْبِهٖ أَجْمَعِيْنَ

بِسْمِ اللّٰهِ الرَّحْمٰنِ الرَّحِيْمِ

Contents

Fiqh

Water

1. List 5 types of water that can be used in order to become pure.

1. rain water
2. tap water
3. sea water
4. well water
5. flowing water

2. What must water be in order for it to be used for wuḍū‘ and ghusl?

It must be pure.

3. Which one of the following amounts of water is classified as a large quantity? Tick the correct answers.

12m x 12m (circled) | 7m x 2.5m | 3m | $25m^2$ (circled)

4. When would water be classified as impure?

If it is dirty.

5. When is water regarded as used?

When you have done wudu with it.

Fiqh

Water

Yaḥya wants to perform wuḍū' for ṣalāh whilst out on a picnic. Help him understand the rulings regarding impurities falling into large quantities of water. Relate to the smell, taste and colour changing.

Create an infographic outlining these points in a simple and clear way.

WATER

Water ways

→ Water must be pure

→ water must be clean

HW

Impurities

Give 5 examples of heavy impurities.

blood

urine

dirty water

animals

animals blood

Give three examples of light impurities.

~~Colour~~ siliver

~~tested~~ water

~~smell~~ dogs'siliver

Impurities

HW

Design a poster showing the different amounts of impurities that may be present for ṣalāh to be valid or invalid.

IMPURITIES

impurities

- When doing salah you should:
  have clean clothes
  washed your body
  have no body odour

- When doing salah you shouldn't have:
  smelly clothes
  have a smelly body
  have body odour

* Remember when you are praying salah to always be clean! *

HW

Impurities

Explain how to remove impurities from the following materials and items.

Carpet

use vanish and scrub the stain

Bucket

use soap and water to scrub

Table

use anti-bacterial spray and wipe

Mattress

use water and soap and squeeze the mattress

Cloth

wash in washing machine

Maturity

Create an information leaflet detailing all the aspects relating to maturity.

Maturity

head	start	clean	sprinkle	half
the	nose	mouth	the	nostrils
entire	top	rinse	wash	body
finish	the	wrist	rinse	

In your own words, write down points that you have learnt about making ghusl.

Maturity

Fill in the blanks

nifās	blood	three	istiḥāḍah
month	less	ḥayḍ	

As a girl matures, her body develops and changes take place. One of these changes is the releasing of __________ from the vagina. There are three types of blood which are released, ḥayḍ, __________ and __________. Blood which flows every __________ from the private part is called ḥayḍ. The minimum period of ḥayḍ is __________ days and the maximum is 10 days. Blood which flows __________ than 3 days or more than 10 days will be regarded as istiḥāḍah. A woman will not get __________ before the age of 9. Any blood before the age of 9 will be regarded as istiḥāḍah.

Mention 4 things that are not permitted during ḥayḍ and nifās.

1.

2.

3.

4.

Maturity

Make a calendar with 4 days shaded.
Show the following examples in the calendar below by shading and labelling the relevant boxes.

Scenario 1
Āminah began her ḥayḍ on the 2nd of the month. She had the minimum amount of ḥayḍ and minimum amount of ṭuhr.

Scenario 2
Ḥalīmah's ḥayḍ began on the 5th of the month. She had the maximum amount of ḥayḍ and thereafter, she began bleeding on the 23rd of the month. What will this blood be classified as and when is the earliest date her next ḥayḍ can start?

Scenario 3
Salma began bleeding on the 10th of the month, 15 days after her last ḥayḍ. She saw no blood for the next three days. On the morning of the 14th she started bleeding again. What will these days be classed as?

Scenario 4
Khadījah's normal ḥayḍ is six days. This month she saw blood for 13 days. State which days will be classed as ḥayḍ and istiḥāḍah.

Scenario 5
Zīnat's normal ḥayḍ is 5 days. This month she saw blood for 10 days. What will this blood be classed as?

Wājib acts in Ṣalāh

Complete the pie chart by explaining the titles.

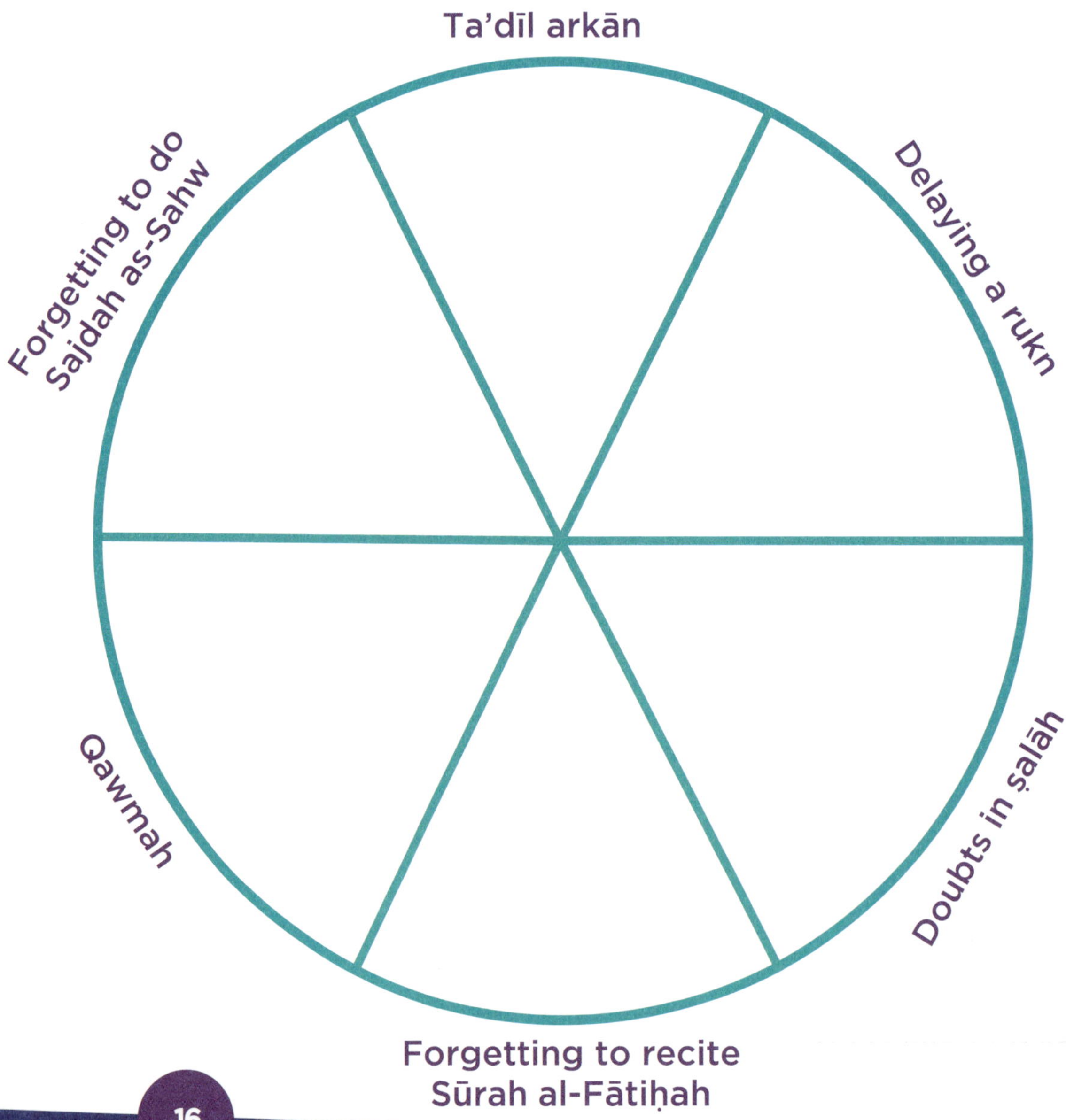

Janāzah

jewellery	**hair**	**massage**
clothing	**water**	**wuḍū'**
mouth		

Do not comb or cut the ____________ of the deceased or clip their nails but remove all ____________, any dentures etc.

Cover the private area with a cloth. Remove all ____________ including underwear by cutting.

Block nostrils, ears and ____________ with cotton wool to prevent ____________ entering during ghusl.

Wearing gloves but without looking, ____________ the stomach gently and wash both private parts. Wash away any najāsah which comes out.

Perform ____________ on the deceased without pouring water into the deceased's nostrils or mouth.

Janāzah

Role play 1

Rābiah has passed away and her body needs to be washed and prepared for burial. In this role-play, you need to wash her body.

You will need a towel, sheet, soap, jug and cotton wool.

Using an appropriate prop (dummy or log). You are to practice doing the ghusl for the deceased. Split into groups consisting of approximately 6 students.

Take a role:

1. Main Washer – taking the lead
2. Somebody who will be reading out the instructions
3. Assistants (x4)

Task

Prepare a small booklet detailing the process of preparing a body for burial. Include the following points:

1. Method of washing the body
2. How to shroud the body
3. The method of performing Janāzah Ṣalāh

What you will need:

1. A4 paper
2. Scissors
3. Pens and pencils
4. Colouring pencils
5. Stapler

Some of this can be provided by your teacher.

Janāzah

Role play 2

Rabia's body has been washed and now it is time to shroud her. In this role-play you will need to correctly shroud her body and prepare it for burial.

You will need some material for the kafan.

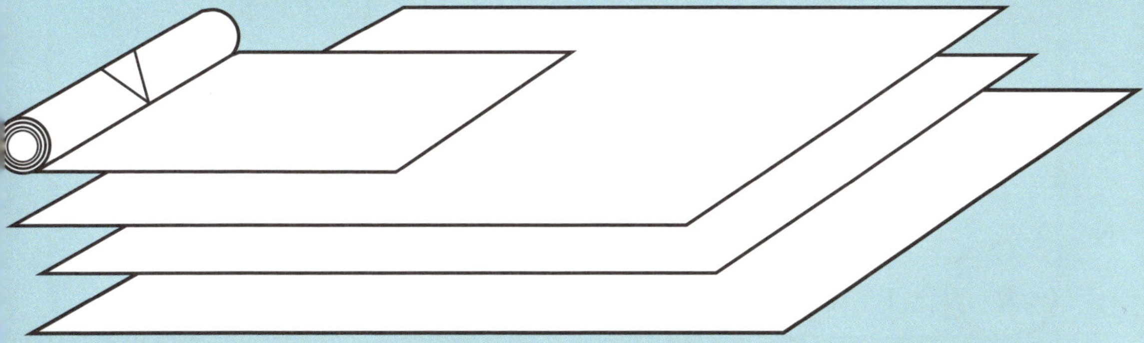

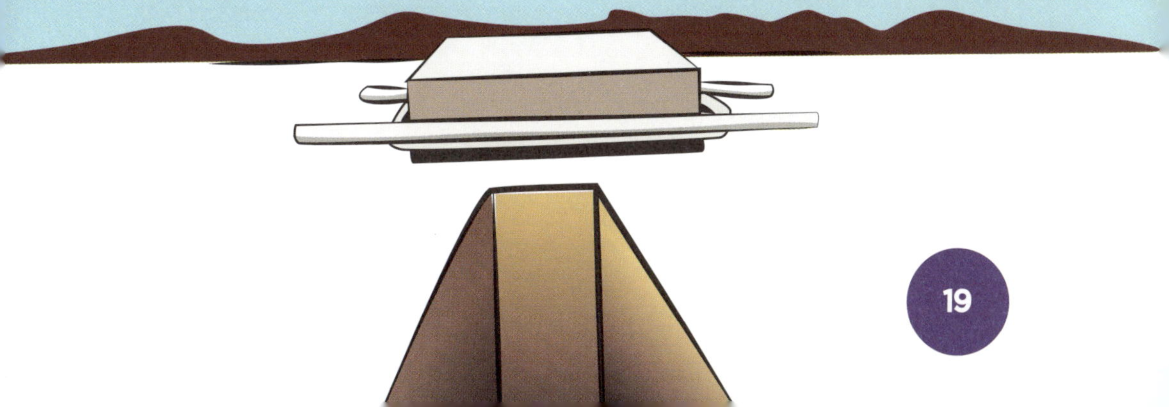

Janāzah

Complete the wordseach

Temporary	Īmān	Punishment
Qiblah	Kalimah	Deceased
Janāzah	Ghusl	Kafan
Lifāfah	Qamīs	Izār
Khirkah	Khimār	Camphor

S	J	H	H	I	S	P	D	J	L	M	N	Q	Q	L
H	E	O	X	U	A	U	S	Q	B	A	N	J	D	G
A	Q	E	J	X	B	N	I	N	M	Y	J	I	E	T
Z	I	C	Y	R	V	I	M	I	E	V	W	D	E	U
A	B	P	Z	D	E	S	A	E	C	E	D	M	T	K
N	L	S	U	H	G	H	Q	H	N	S	P	X	H	O
A	A	K	N	M	E	M	C	C	A	O	F	I	E	R
J	H	F	U	Q	U	E	U	A	R	M	M	C	G	S
X	I	Z	A	R	E	N	T	A	M	A	I	H	Z	V
J	Q	H	J	K	S	T	R	A	R	P	A	L	F	L
Y	X	Z	K	V	K	Y	C	H	M	F	H	O	A	P
K	H	I	R	K	A	H	A	A	A	E	G	O	Y	K
T	V	G	L	B	L	W	J	F	E	V	T	R	R	Q
Q	C	P	I	L	H	U	I	U	C	Q	A	L	M	R
R	N	I	E	A	V	L	K	C	J	D	U	Z	M	N

Fill in the blanks.

The Janāzah Ṣalāh is in reality a du'ā' for the ________.
There is no _______ or Sajdah.
There are _______ takbīrāt in the Janāzah Ṣalāh.

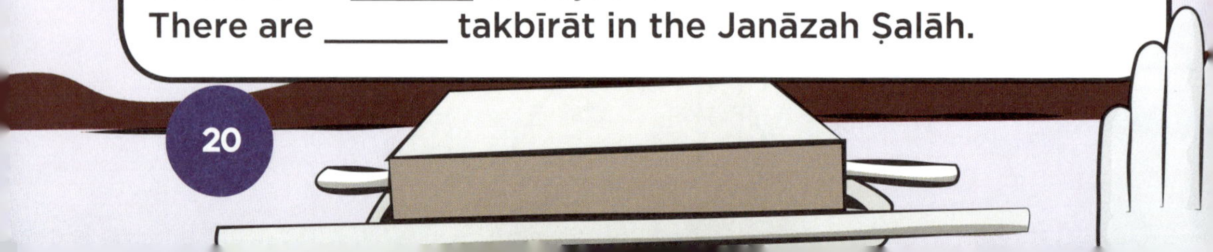

Janāzah

Answer the questions below.

What should be done after the first takbīr?

What must the congregation not do during the second takbīr?

What must we recite after the second takbīr?

During the third takbīr what will the congregation not do?

After they say the third takbīr what will they recite?

During the fourth takbīr what must the congregation not do?

What will happen after the fourth takbīr?

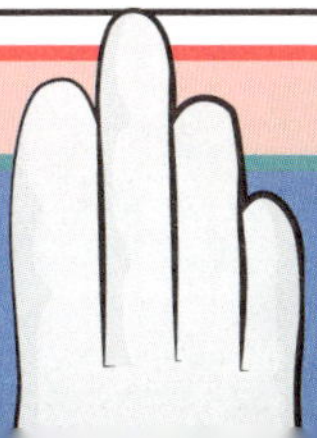

Aḥādīth

Copy out the Arabic text of the first four aḥādīth in the boxes below then write 2 things that you learn from that ḥadīth.

listening to your parents
- obeying them
- respecting them

Being beautiful
- showing beauty
- being beautiful

Dis-obeying
- disobeying your parent
- being rude

Shirk
- accosiating partners with allah
- not believing in allah.

Major Sins

How did the Prophet صلى الله عليه وسلم respond when he was asked what the major sins were?

1. Shirk
2. dis-Obeying
3. Killing
4. having arrogance/false testomony

Pride

What did our Beloved Messenger Muḥammad صلى الله عليه وسلم say about having pride in the heart even if it is the size of a mustard seed?

You will not enter Jannah.

What did our Beloved Messenger Muḥammad صلى الله عليه وسلم say about beauty?

Make the effects of the blessing and grace of Allah appear on you.

Good Character

Fill in the blanks

The Beloved Messenger Muhammad صلى الله عليه وسلم **said:**

Surely I was sent **to perfect the** qualities **of righteous** character.

Health and Free Time

According to the ḥadīth, what are the two things people fail to make the most of?

Circle the correct two answers and discuss it with a partner.

Good Health (circled)	Lots of Money
Parents (circled)	Free Time
Lots of sleep	

Truth and Lies

Write out the translation of the ḥadīth about truth leading to goodness.

verily truth will guide you to goodness and good leaves to Jannah (heaven).

Love for the Messenger صلى الله عليه وسلم

Research on one of the following topics from the life of our Beloved Messenger Muḥammad صلى الله عليه وسلم and write an article about it. Remember to support the facts with examples from his blessed life.

His character
His favours upon the ummah
His physical description
His social interaction

Five Pillars

Design your own crossword on the pillars of Islām. Make the questions challenging and once completed, ask a fellow student to find the answers.

Qur'ān

How will reading the Qur'ān help you on the Day of Judgement?

Write down the importance of the Qur'ān

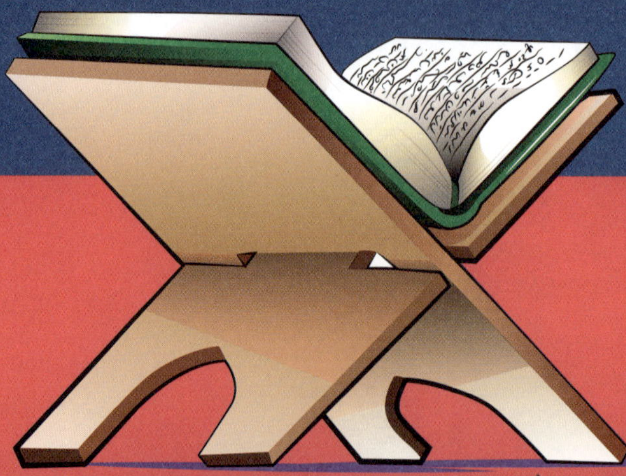

Ṣalāh

Complete the images below by writing the numbers on the clocks and then note down the ṣalāh times for tomorrow using the masjid timetable.

Fajr

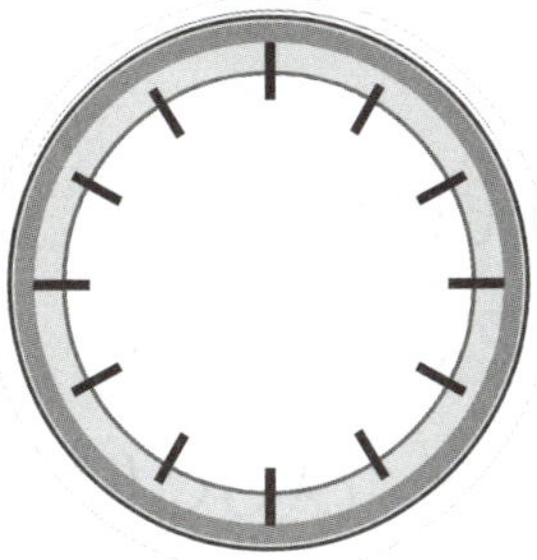

Time: ____________

Ẓuhr

Time: ____________

'Aṣr

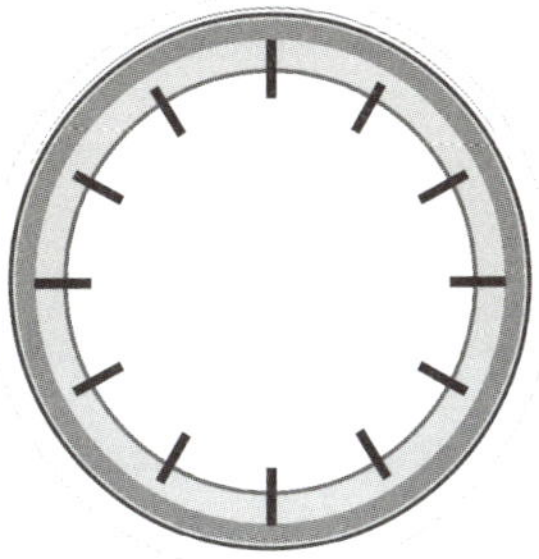

Time: ____________

Maghrib

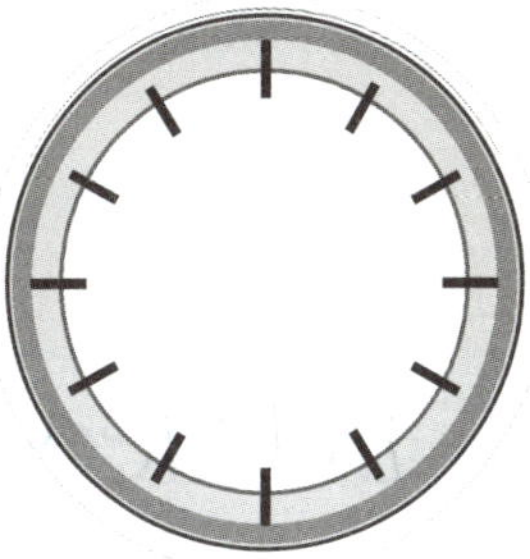

Time: ____________

'Ishā'

Time: ____________

CW → HW

Kindness to Parents

Ahadīth

Locate three 'rabbanā' du'ā's in the Qur'ān, write them down in Arabic with the translation, and memorise them.

Discuss why Islām gives importance to respecting one's parents. Make notes of your discussion below.

Respecting your parents is very important because one out of the 7 doors of Jannah you will enter. if you help your parents mentally, physically, finacially.

Gatherings

The beloved **Messenger Muḥammad** صلى الله عليه وسلم **said:**

Whenever a ______ gathers for ____________ Allāh, Mighty and ___________ is He, angels ________ them (Divine) mercy _______ them, tranquillity ________ upon them, and Allāh ________ them to those (angels) in His presence.'

Good Actions

We have been reminded that every act of goodness is charity. Over the next week, record ten acts of goodness you do and at the end of each day reflect upon them. When you meet again as a class, work with a partner and share your experiences with each other.

1. ____

2. ____

3. ____

4. ____

5. ____

6. ____

7. ____

8. ____

9. ____

10. ____

Ṣadaqah

Design a motivational money box sticker for a local charitable cause. Once completed, stick it on a money box. Use the space provided to sketch some ideas.

Ramaḍān

Experiment:

Work in a group
You will need
- a bowl of water
- 3 drops of oil

Instructions:

Put three drops of oil into the water.

Write down the link between your experiment and the act of fasting in the month of Ramaḍān.

____
____
____
____
____

In your own words write down the ḥadīth about the reward of fasting in Ramaḍān.

____
____
____
____
____
____

Friendship

Ādam has recently made friends with wrong people. Write a message to Ādam advising him to keep good company. Use your knowledge and the following ḥadith to persuade him.

"A person tends to follow the faith (and lifestyle) of his friends, so be careful who you make friends with."

Work with a partner and challenge each other to learn all the aḥādīth. See who can repeat them all correctly in the shortest amount of time. Use the box below to note down your times for each attempt.

Sīrah

Shamā'il

A syllable is a part of a word which is pronounced as a unit. It is normally made up of a vowel alone or a vowel with one or more consonants. For instance the word "Haiku" has two syllables: Hai-ku; the word "introduction" has four syllables: in-tro-duc-tion.

"Haiku" is a traditional form of Japanese poetry. Each haiku poem consists of 3 lines in total. The first and last lines of a Haiku have 5 syllables and the middle line has 7 syllables. The lines do not have to rhyme.

Write five different Haikus based on the Shamā'il of the Prophet Muḥammad صلى الله عليه وسلم.

Apperance
Journey

footsteps

Appearance-
what he looks
like

biograpny-
info

naiku

Shamā'il

List 10 things you have learnt about the Prophet صلى الله عليه وسلم's appearance

1. unique
2. Jet black
3. eyes
4. wavy hair
5. middle parts
6. big eyes
7. good body
8. long hair
9. long baird
10. average height

Abū Bakr رضي الله عنه

Using a dictionary, find out the meaning of 'genealogy.'

a line of descendent traced continously from an ancestor.

Early life

Complete the word search below.

P	T	H	L	E	M	A	M	G	X
Y	D	S	B	A	B	A	Y	V	Z
Z	G	I	E	U	C	Y	A	O	A
L	R	O	B	N	A	J	T	T	S
T	Z	A	L	M	O	O	U	S	S
J	K	R	N	A	Y	H	N	U	I
R	O	D	L	Q	E	J	A	R	D
G	L	U	V	L	L	N	B	T	D
H	S	Y	A	R	U	Q	E	L	I
G	E	N	E	R	O	U	S	G	Q

Abū Bakr رضي الله عنه
Genealogy
Trust
Tribe
Banū Taym
Honest
Generous
Quraysh
Businessman
~~As-Siddīq~~

Abū Bakr رضي الله عنه

Sīrah

What great qualities did Abū Bakr رضي الله عنه posses?

he was very kind
noblemen LOVED HIM

Looking at the text about Abū Bakr رضي الله عنه, list 5 points you have learnt about him before he accepted Islām.

1. never drank
2. was sensible
3. was kind
4. searching truth
5. Shared happiness

Abū Bakr رضي الله عنه

Circle the names of those Ṣaḥābah who were invited to Islām by Abū Bakr رضي الله عنه.

Sa'd ibn Abī Waqqās

Al Arqam ibn Abil Arqam

Lubābah bint al-Ḥārith

Talḥah ibn 'Ubaydullāh

Abd al-Rahman ibn Awf

Bilāl ibn Rabāḥ

Zubayr ibn al-'Awwām

'Uthmān ibn Madh'ūn

Khabbab ibn al-Aratt

'Abdullāh ibn Mas'ūd

Ja'far ibn Abī Ṭālib

Abū 'Ubaydah ibn Al Jarrāḥ

Sa'd ibn Abī Waqqās

'Uthmān ibn Affān

Khālid ibn Sa'īd

Abū Salamah ibn 'Abdul As'ad

Abū Bakr رضي الله عنه

Answer the following questions

Sīrah

1. For the first three years how was the call to Islām made?

____

____

2. What happened when Abū Bakr رضي الله عنه gave a sermon in Masjid Al Ḥarām?

____

____

____

____

____

____

Abū Bakr رضي الله عنه

Fill in the blanks

After facing much __________ from the disbelievers of ________, Allāh سبحانه وتعالى made a way for the Believers. He placed ______ in the heart of the people of Madīnah ________, they came for three ______ consecutively accepting īmān and _________ the message in their city. They then ____________ their innermost wish: to have the ________ Messenger صلى الله عليه وسلم and the _________ come and reside in Madīnah Munawwarah and so _____ to this blessed ______ began. Abū Bakr رضي الله عنه prepared to ______ with others that were _________ but the Beloved Messenger صلى الله عليه وسلم requested him to wait until Allāh سبحانه وتعالى granted the Prophet صلى الله عليه وسلم a ______ companion. Abū Bakr رضي الله عنه understood that this ___________ might very well be himself.

Abū Bakr رضي الله عنه

Draw and label a map detailing the journey of Hijrah.

Abū Bakr رضي الله عنه

Why did Abū Bakr رضي الله عنه immediately vomit after he ate some food?

On the plate below, write the things that you should look out for in order to make sure that the food you're eating is ḥalāl.

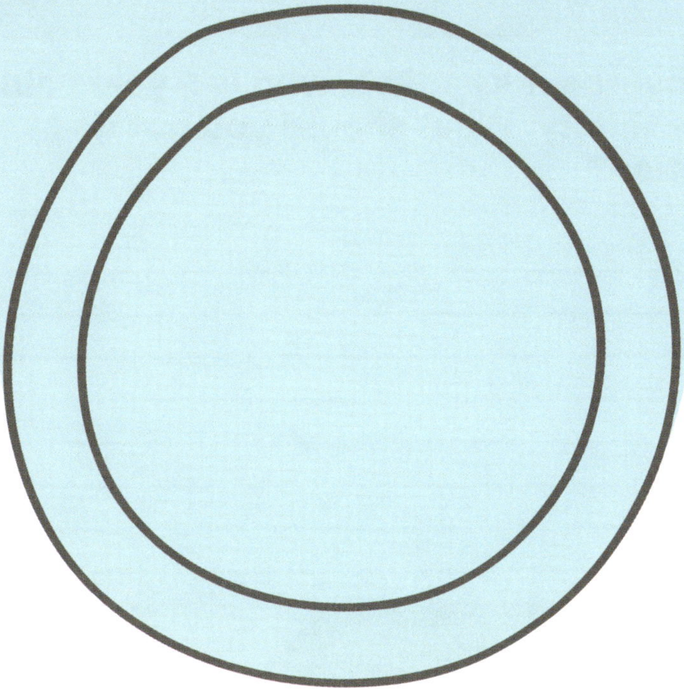

Finding Opportunities to do a Good Deed.

'Ārifah and 'Aqīlah are walking home. It is dark and they have noticed an elderly woman who has dropped her shopping bags on the floor. What should they do in this situation?

You overhear Khadījah, who is 5 years old, saying she is thirsty. What should you not do in this situation?

Finding Opportunities to do a Good Deed.

Sīrah

As you are walking down a street you notice there is a banana skin on the floor. At this moment what can you do that will please Allāh سبحانه وتعالى?

____

____

____

____

What are the three things according to the ḥadīth, when found in a person, would grant them entry into Jannah?

1.______________________________

____

2.______________________________

____

3.______________________________

____

The Mothers of the Believers

Make notes as you study the lives of the Mothers of the Believers then create a set of flash cards. On one side write their respective names using Arabic calligraphy. On the reverse, note down five key points from their lives.

Select one of the Mothers of the Believers and prepare a short speech about her life. Deliver your speech to the class.

The Mothers of the Believers

Research and create a small booklet containing key points from the lives of the Mothers of the Believers.

Tārīkh

Dāwūd & Sulaymān عليهما السلام

Circle the correct answer.
T = True or F = False

1. Dāwūd عليه السلام besides being brave and wise, was known for his wonderful voice, which he used to sing the praises of Allāh سبحانه وتعالى.	T / F
2. When he recited the praises of Allāh سبحانه وتعالى the mountains and birds would not like it and cry.	T / F
3. Dāwūd عليه السلام remained a humble servant of Allāh سبحانه وتعالى.	T / F
4. Only a large sip of water using a jug was allowed.	T / F
5. Jālūt was the slave of his people.	T / F
6. The most beloved fasting to Allāh سبحانه وتعالى was that of Dāwūd عليه السلام, who used to fast on alternate days.	T / F

Dāwūd & Sulaymān عليهما السلام

Tārīkh

Find the following verse in the Qur'ān.

""O mountains, pronounce with him Allāh's purity repeatedly - and you too O birds!" And We made the iron soft for him saying to him, "Make coats of armour, and maintaian balance in combining rings, and all of you do, righteous deeds. Surely I am watchful of what you do."' (34:10-11)

What are the Arabic words for:

1. Birds altuyur
2. Iron hadid
3. Armour dire
4. Watchful yaqiz

What was the special gift given to Dāwūd عليه السلام **according to this verse?**

The gift was the iron soft voice.

Dāwūd & Sulaymān عليهما السلام

Complete the crossword below.

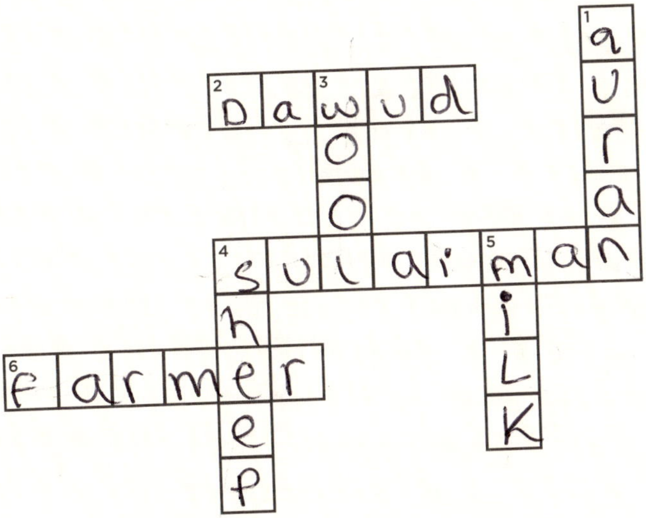

Across
2. - He defeated Jalūt.
4. - The son of Dāwūd عليه السلام.
6. - A person who cultivates land.

Down
1. - A book revealed through Jibra'īl.
3. - The fine, soft curly hair forming the coat of a sheep.
4. - A farm animal with a thick woolly coat.
5. - A white liquid rich in fat and protein.

Dāwūd & Sulaymān عليهما السلام

Fill in the blanks

"And for Sulaymān (We subjugated) the _______. Its journey in the ________ was (equal to the journey of) one _______, and its journey in the _________ was (equal to the journey) of another month. And We caused a ______ of copper to_____ for him. And there were some _______ who worked before him with the _______ of his Lord. Whoever of them would deviate from Our _______, We would make him taste the ____________ of the Blazing _____. They used to make for him whatever he wished of _______, images, basins as (large as) tanks, and large cookware fixed (in their places). "Be thankful O family of __________. Very few from My slaves are thankful." (34:12-13).

One day ___________ عليه السلام was travelling with his army when he passed a valley of ______. One of the ants ________ the other ants of the coming ______ saying:
'O ants, enter your dwelling places so that Sulaymān and his armies don't ______ you unknowingly.' So he (Sulaymān) smiled, laughing on her speech and said, "My Lord, enable me to become grateful to Your favour that You have bestowed on me and on my __________, and to do good deeds that You like, and admit me, with Your ______, among Your righteous servants."

Dāwūd & Sulaymān عليهما السلام

After you have filled in the blanks, look back at the two paragraphs above and count how many times the following words appear. Tally your findings.

We	3/|||
Ants	3/|||
And	5/|||||

Dāwūd & Sulaymān عليهما السلام

Tārīkh

Find the following verse in the Qur'ān and write it in Arabic.

"And (once) he (Sulaymān) checked the birds and said, "How is it with me that I do not see the hudhud (hoopoe)? Rather he has disappeared. I will punish him with a severe punishment or slaughter him unless he brings to me a clear proof." (27:20-21)

وَتَفَقَّدَ ٱلطَّيْرَ فَقَالَ
قَالِ لَآ أَرَى ٱلْهُدْهُدَ ۝

Dāwūd & Sulaymān عليهما السلام

Write a letter to your friend informing them of what had happened with the hoopoe and the Queen of Sheba. Remember to include as much detail as possible.

the hoopoe was a bird and he saw the prophets army and all of them hid

the queen wanted to bribe the phrophet. and became muslim

Tārīkh

Dāwūd & Sulaymān عليهما السلام

Using a dictionary find the meanings of the following words.

Deviate
____

Specific
____

Severe
____

Throne
____

Esteemed
____

Envoy
____

Extend
____

Humiliation
____

Bountiful
____

Submit
____

Dāwūd & Sulaymān عليهما السلام

Now find the words in the text and write out the sentence they appear in.

Yūnus عليه السلام

1. Work with a partner. In the Qur'ān find this verse in Sūrah al-Inshirāḥ and then write out the Arabic text.

'Verily after hardship there will be ease.'

naqana baed almashaqat
yakun hunak raha

Tārīkh

2. Which people did Allāh سبحانه وتعالى send Yūnus عليه السلام to?

nineveh

3. What did Yūnus عليه السلام ask the people to do?

convert to islam

4. What did the people of Nineveh do before the punishment came to them?

behave bad with Prophet yunus.

5. How did the people decide who was to be thrown into the sea?

Yūnus عليه السلام

What was the du'ā' that Yūnus عليه السلام made?

there is no god but you pare are you indeed was among the wrongdoers

What happened after Yūnus عليه السلام made this du'ā'?

allah let the phroph-et yunus to tell the whale to put him on the ground

Can you think of a time when you were really worried? What happened and what did you do?

no, i can't!

Find Spain. Circle it.
Then find China and circle it too.

Islamic History

Relating to Islamic history what can you explain about these two countries?

Now put a circle around where Damascus is.

The Umayyads

Research into the following, and write what you have found out about them.

1. Umayyad Khilāfah:

____

____

____

____

____

____

____

____

____

____

2. Mu'āwiyah رضي الله عنه:

____

____

____

____

____

____

____

____

____

____

The Umayyads

3. Marwān ibn 'Abdul Malik:

4. 'Umar ibn 'Abdul 'Azīz:

The Umayyads

Design a poster using the information you have gathered from the section 'Contributions to the World'.

The Umayyads

For your homework find out how many countries in the world use Arabic as their official language. List them below:

‘Aqā’id

Ahlus Sunnah Wal Jamā'ah

Define Ahlus Sunnah Wal Jamā'ah:

This is the stages of sunni
muslim.

In the circles below write the following in order of succession:

1. Tābi'ūn
2. Ṣaḥābah
3. Taba' Tābi'īn

Sahābah

Tāb'ūn

baba'/
TĀbl'īn

'Aqā'id

Ahlus Sunnah Wal Jamā'ah

In each square below write and explain the three main sections when discussing Aqā'id.

Believe in god.

Belief in islami-c holy book

Belief in phrophets and messeng-ers

'Aqā'id

Nabawiyyāt

Using the information about the prophets write a 5-line poem using alliteration.

A short example has been done for you.

A rasūl is rare and really respected by his followers.
A nabī received revelations rightly reminding people of the truth.

Nabawiyyāt

Compare the difference between a nabī and a rasūl.

Who was a nabī ordered to follow?

Find out how many prophets have been mentioned in the Qur'ān.

HW

The Qualities of the Prophets

Unscramble the following words.

S N M U H A

h u m a n s

T N E S O H

h o n e s t

L L E E N N T T I I G

i n t e l l i g e n t

U R T S W T H R Y O T

t r u s t w o R t H Y

'Aqā'id

The Qualities of the Prophets

HW

Write an article about the qualities of the prophets. Remember to include sections relating to:

1) ‘Iṣmah
2) ‘Iṣṭifa’
3) Waḥy

all the prophets that are mentioned in the quran and all the other prophets are free from sin, they are choosen by allah and they recieve revolution (wahi).

HW

The Qualities of the Prophets

Write the following words out in Braille.

The Braille Alphabet

A	B	C	D	E	F	G	H	I	J

K	L	M	N	O	P	Q	R	S	T

U	V	W	X	Y	Z

1) **The Angel Jibra'īl.**

istifah

2) **The Divine Message.**

ismah

3) **The Revelation.**

wahi

Which pages are these words on?

The Ṣaḥābah

Design a poster based on the ranks of the Ṣaḥābah.

SAHABAH

the four Khulafa rashidun

Asharah mushrah

battle of badr

battle of uhud

pledged bayan al ridwan

The Ṣaḥābah

Write the name 'Abū Bakr' رضي الله عنه in Arabic bubble writing and decorate it.

ابو بكر

Abū Bakr رضي
الله عنه

'Aqā'id

The Ṣaḥābah

In one paragraph write five things you know about 'Uthmān رضي الله عنه.

uthman was the son in law of the phrophet muhamad swt. He is also a martyr.

'Aqā'id

The Ṣaḥābah

Who was the second Khalīfah?

umar

How many years younger was he than the Beloved Prophet صلى الله عليه وسلم?

When did he accept Islām?

What can you explain about his rank?

He is the second Khulafa and also a father in law to the prophet muhammad swt.

The Ṣaḥābah

Write a 'who am I' riddle for the four separate Ṣaḥābah. Each riddle must be a minimum of five lines long. Once completed give your riddles to someone in your class and see if they can figure out which Companion you have written about.

Remember to:

- Try to use the present tense more
- Make it challenging!
- Begin each sentence with a capital letter and end it with a full-stop, question mark or exclamation mark.
- Finish with the question – Who am I?

The Ṣaḥābah

1. who met the prophet muhammad in a state of imān and passed away with islam.

2. the four khulafa rashidun

3. Asharah Mubasharah

4. battle of badr and the battle of uhud. pledged bayah al ridwan.

'Aqā'id

The 'Asharah Mubasharah

Cut up ten pieces of card 5cm x 8cm. On each card write a different name of those Ṣaḥābah who were promised Jannah in one gathering. Design the cards with calligraphy or colour.

Now work with a partner playing 'guess who'.

1. Mix the cards up and place them upside-down in a pile.
2. Pick up the top card and read the first name of the Ṣaḥābī.
3. Your partner must tell you the Ṣaḥābī's father's name.
4. If you read one of the cards with the names of Abū Bakr, 'Umar, 'Uthmān or 'Alī رضي الله عنهم then your partner must tell you which khalīfāh they were.
5. If your partner gets it right they keep the card, if they get it wrong then it goes to the bottom of the pile.
6. The person with the most cards wins the game.

'Aqā'id

Write down what you've learnt about the friends of Allāh سبحانه وتعالى.

Mu'jizāt

Activity:
Describing and explaining the miracles

Work in a group and write on separate pieces of paper:

a. The miracle of Ṣāliḥ عليه السلام
b. The miracle of Ibrāhīm عليه السلام
c. The miracle of Mūsā عليه السلام
d. The miracles of 'Īsā عليه السلام
e. The miracles of the Prophet Muḥammad صلى الله عليه وسلم

Then using a newspaper make a 'pass the parcel' game, and in between each layer of newspaper place the 'miracles' sheets of paper. As soon as the teacher says 'stop', the person who is holding the parcel at that time will unwrap a layer and list the miracles of that prophet.

The parcel must not move again to the next person until all the miracles have been remembered. Other group members can help in this.

The Miracles of Prophet Muḥammad صلى الله عليه وسلم

Design a poster showing one of the greatest miracles of the Prophet Muḥammad صلى الله عليه وسلم.

The Miracles of Prophet Muḥammad صلى الله عليه وسلم

List the other miracles performed by our Beloved Messenger Muḥammad صلى الله عليه وسلم.

Give an example of a karāmah of Maryam رضي الله عنها.

____

____

____

____

____

____

____

Fill in the blanks

The ___________ between a mu'jizah and a ___________ is that a mu'jizah is done by a ___________ as a result of a challenge. A karāmah is not done as a _______ of a challenge.

Al-Isrā' and Al-Mi'rāj

Create your own word search using the following words. You may ask someone to find the words once you have completed it.

Isrā'
Mi'rāj
Makkah
Jibra'īl
Mikā'īl
Burāq
Jerusalem
Aqṣā
Heaven
Qur'ān
Journey

Now add 3 words of your own from the story.

1. ____________

2. ____________

3. ____________

Activity!

Now give your word search to someone else in the class. See how many words they can find.

Al-Isrā' and Al-Mi'rāj

Using the words from the word search write up a summary of what happened during the night journey of Al-Isrā' Wal-Mi'rāj

Akhlāq

HW

Oppression & Bullying

Explain the two opening āyāt from the topic of oppression and bullying.

1. Never think that god is unaware of what the wrong-does are doing, He is but giving them respite up to a day when the eyes shall remain upraised

2. Our beloved messenger said: "oppression will turn into darkness on the day of resurrection Sāhih-āl-Bukhārī.

Complete the following sentences:

Allāh سبحانه وتعالى does not like any type of oppression and His punishment for the oppressors will be

Oppression in Arabic is known as "ظلم" ظلمات ظلماً ظلما

The definition of ẓulm is putting something in the incorrect place.

Oppression & Bullying

Make an anti-bullying keyring.

In the box below draw what your keyring looks like.

Oppression & Bullying

Using A4 paper draw 6 triangles with each line being 7cm long. In each triangle write a word which shows kindness and good character. You may decorate this and make it colourful. At the top of each triangle, using a hole punch make holes for the string to be passed through. Now you have completed your bunting.

See the example below.

Akhlāq

Oppression & Bullying

Role play

Hold a class discussion with your teacher on the reasons people bully others and why they are wrong to do so.

Imagine you are going live on radio as a group. One person needs to be the host, the other two will answer questions. You may swap roles if there is time.

Prepare an interview script that the host will use to ask questions to the two guests about how they felt whilst they were being bullied.

While I was being bullied, I felt angry and upset all I wanted to do was shout and scream. But I couldn't if I did they would have done something to me. But, I didn't care what they had to say and I told them to leave me alone.

Akhlāq

Oppression & Bullying

Answer the following

If Aḥmed picks on Bilāl, how do you think Bilāl will feel?

upset, furios and mad.

Khadījah purposely leaves ʻĀʼishah out of a game. How do you think Khadījah has made ʻĀʼishah feel?

mad and left out.

Fill in the blanks.

In another Ḥadīth Qudsī Allāh سبحانه وتعالى says:
"He who against enmity against my order, I (Allāh) will war against him!" Think! The person you are hurting and taunting today, could be the servant of Allāh! What chance do you have against the ruler of all kings?
Repent to do today and apologise to all those you have hurt and promise not to hurt anyone again.

Oppression & Bullying

Work in groups of four and discuss the following scenarios. Write down the discussion points below.

Scenario 1:

Rumaysah, Nuṣaybah and Madīḥah are good friends. One day Rumaysah and Madīḥah have an argument with Nuṣaybah. They pick on her and cause her harm whilst she is in school. Nusayba becomes very upset.

What should Nuṣaybah do in order to resolve the issue between them all?

She should leave them alone because they have a problem in their life and their getting it out on her. She should also tell someone such as a teacher/parent or guardian.

Oppression & Bullying

Scenario 2:

Muḥammad and Fahīm are partners on the bus and are going on a school trip. Fahīm notices his other friend Yūsuf to the side of him and spends all day talking to him and ignoring Muḥammad. Muḥammad feels upset and sad.

You are on the trip and notice Muḥammad being left out. What should you do?

I would talk to him and I would comfort him.

What does the word oppression mean?

prolonged cruel or unjust treatment or exercise of authority.

What is the difference between oppression and bullying?

Oppresion means to be cruel and bullying means to be rude constantly.

Oppression & Bullying

Retell the story of the beggar in your own words. Remember you are not to copy it word for word.

There was a begger that came to a rich man's house asking for scraps. The wife was willing to give him some, but on the other hand the husband didn't and he kicked him. Years later, the rich man became bamkrupt and he had no choice but to divorce with his wife. The wife married the beggar and they had a happy family. The rich man became a beggar and went to the beggars house and asked for scraps. the wife said no but the beggear didn't.

Musa

HW

Envy

Find the following verse in the Qur'ān and read it in Arabic.

"Or, is it that they are envious of people over what Allāh has given them of His bounty..." (Qur'ān 4:54)

Use a dictionary and find out the meaning of envy.

Jelous

Write a descriptive story on the topic of envy.

there were two birds and they both liked eachother but one of them liked the other one so they went to a islamic bird scholar and he helped one bird.

Envy

Write out the following sentences correctly. The words have been mixed up and some extra words have been added.

Not I jump envy fire the first sin then committed Earth in because the Heavens and punishment the and first now sin wanted was committed on why.

Write the accurate sentence below.

the first sin was commited on earth and the heavens and punishments.

As if Wanted Qābil they brother envious become of own his three Hābil wondered which brother led school him to because murder his chose.

Write the accurate sentence below.

who gave qabil the choice to murder his brother.

☆ **What are the five things Allāmah Faqih Samarqandi** رحمه الله **stated that envious people suffer from?**

Akhlāq

Envy

Explain the incident that took place with ‘Abdullāh ibn ‘Amr رضي الله عنه

What is the wonderful cure from envy?

Circle the two sūrahs which have been prescribed for protection from the envious.

Sūrah al-Mulk

Sūrah al-Falaq

Sūrah an-Nās

Sūrah Yasīn

Sūrah al-Ḥijr

Sūrah ad-Dukhān

Envy

What was the practise of the Prophet صلى الله عليه وسلم when he went to bed every night?

Practise this sunnah every night for the next week.

	Carried Out	Not Carried Out
Monday	✓	
Tuesday	✓	
Wednesday	✓	
Thursday	✓	
Friday	✓	
Saturday	✓	
Sunday	✓	

Envy

At the end of the topic about envy there are three du'ā's mentioned in the aḥādīth. Copy the translation and learn it by heart.

he who harbours emmity against my friend i allah wage war against him
sahih al bukhari

Ghībah

Write 5 expressions that may not be considered as backbiting. There is an example here:
Khadījah said to Laṭīfah that Maryam always greets us in the morning with a nice big smile.

1. when some steals
2. when someone speads evil
3. when someone is rude
4. when someone is haram
5. when someone cheats

Write the meaning of 'Huqūqullāh.'

the rights of allah

Write the meaning of 'Huqūqul 'Ibād.'

the rights of the people

Akhlāq

Ghībah

Using a dictionary find the meaning of the word 'bankrupt.'

when you don't have any money at all in cash or in your bank account.

What did the Prophet صلى الله عليه وسلم say about a muflis?

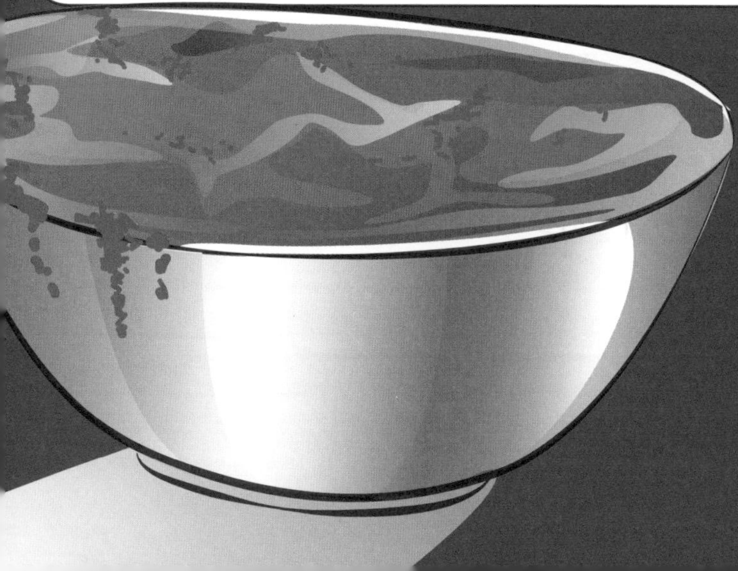

Ghībah

Write two reasons where ghībah is made permissible and under each reason give an example.

Reason 1:
when someone steals

Example:
when someone steals your home.

Reason 2:
when someone spreads evil

Example:
when someone spreads evil you can stop them.

Akhlāq

Ghībah

Complete the ḥadīth:

'The Prophet صلى الله عليه وسلم said, Shall I tell you of that which holds all these things?" I (Mu'ādh) said:

____

____

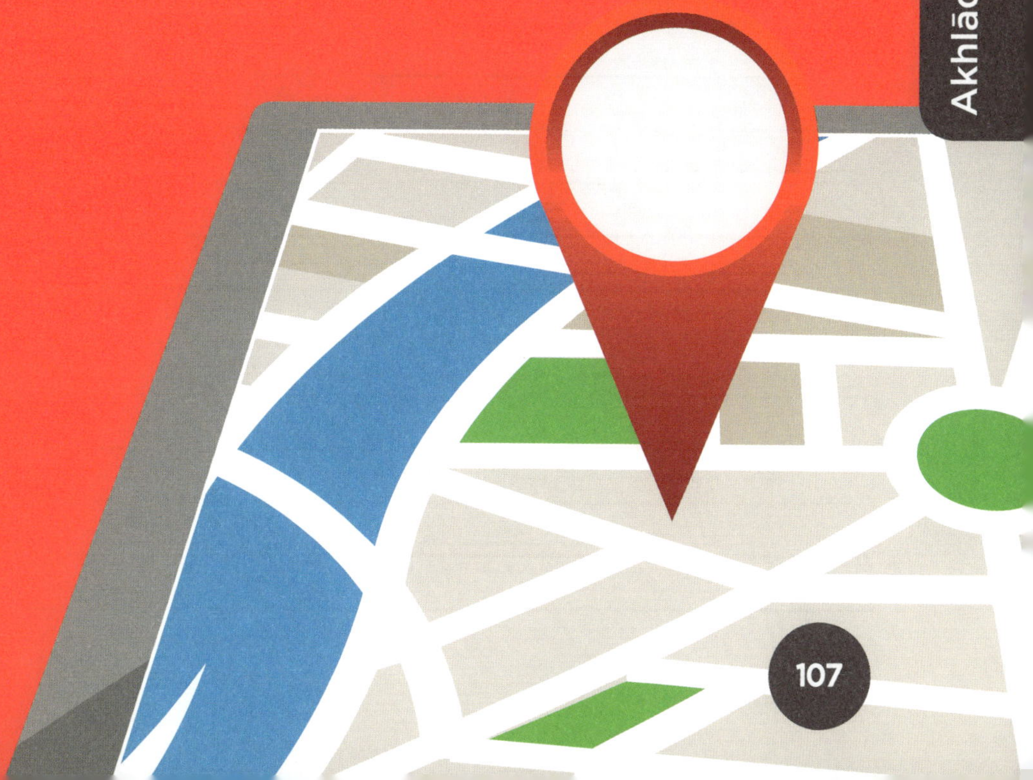

Pride

How did our Beloved Messenger Muḥammad صلى الله عليه وسلم define the word 'pride'?

"rejecting the truth and looking down on people."

Write a story which shows the harms of pride

If you have a single atom of pride in your body you will never enter Jannah.

Akhlāq

Pride

In the Qur'ān, find Sūrah Najm, and read the following verse 53:32.

What was the advice of Shaykh Shihābuddīn Sahrawardi رحمه الله?

before we even think about looking at the faults of others we should take time out and observe ourselves.

After reading the story of Shaykh Abū 'Abdullāh al-Andalusī think of 20 important words that summarise the incident.

1. position
2. avoid
3. piety
4. righteness
5. prominent
6. numerous
7. men
8. heart
9. ahadith
10. recite
11. quran
12. large
13. outskirts
14. prayer
15. begging
16. accepted
17. proposal
18. bowed
19. knowledge
20. heavens

Select ten words from the list and create a word search.

Akhlāq

Pride

Create the word search and ask the person next to you to find the 10 words you chose.

i	s	l	a	m	q	L	m	s	u	v	w	z
d	b	e	t	t	e	r	e	f	j	h	i	g
s	i	n	g	w	i	t	h	m	e	a	b	c
e	w	o	n	t	y	o	p	r	i	d	e	u
c	n	o	o	n	e	n	e	x	t	t	i	m
o	w	l	k	n	o	w	m	y	r	a	h	b
w	e	x	c	e	p	t	x	y	i	z	a	n
l	m	n	o	p	q	r	s	t	g	u	p	v
t	b	c	d	e	f	g	h	l	n	g	p	k
r	a	l	l	a	n	x	y	n	t	z	y	a
u	L	m	n	o	p	q	r	s	t	u	v	w
t	a	b	c	d	e	w	r	o	n	g	e	g
h	a	r	r	o	g	a	n	t	h	i	j	k

1. pride
2. happy
3. wrong
4. right
5. truth
6. better
7. noone
8. except
9. allah
10. arrogant

Akhlāq

Sunnah

Fill in the blank spaces

"Say (O Prophet): 'If you really _____ Allāh, then _____ me, and Allāh shall ____ you and ____ you your sins. Allāh is Most-Forgiving, Very-Merciful.'" (Qur'ān 3: 31)

"Say (O Prophet): 'Obey _____ and the _______.'" (Qur'ān 2:32)

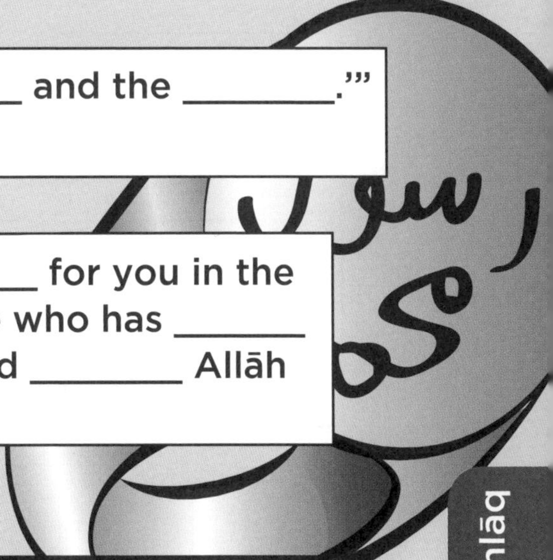

"There is indeed a good ______ for you in the _______ of Allāh - for the one who has ______ in _____ and the Last Day, and _______ Allāh profusely." (Qur'ān 33:21)

Unscramble the word below.

N N A H S U

Write the word here: _ _ _ _ _ _

Explain what this word means.

____

____

Sunnah

Write five points about why we should follow the sunnah.

1.

2.

3.

4.

5.

Now come together as a class and discuss your points together.

Sunnah

Design a card encouraging the use of a miswāk. Use the space below to make a plan. Once you have created your card, share it with pupils from different classes.

Sunnah

Over the next week use a miswāk every morning and night. Record your progress below with the drawing of a miswāk in the correct box.

Day	In the Morning	At night

Sunnah

Research a sunnah of your choice. Using A4 sheets of paper, design snowflakes and write the sunnah in the middle.

Draw a picture of what one of your snowflakes looks like. Remember to include the text also.

What is the reward of holding firm to the sunnah?

___

___

___

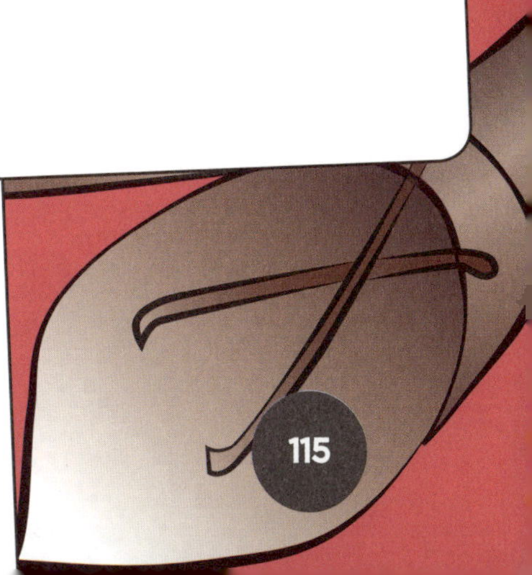

Ādāb

Ādāb of Adhān

Write sentences of how you feel when you hear the adhān.

Locate the words below and write out the sentence in which they appear.

Jinn

Congregational Ṣalāh

Iqāmah

Ādāb of Adhān

Research the story of how the adhān started. Write the story in the space provided.

Ādāb of Adhān

Modesty in Dress

It's World Ḥijāb Day. Your task is to design a pop-up banner to be displayed at the convention. Carry out a survey in your class as part of your research on the benefits of the ḥijāb. Summarise their feelings along with your own in the banner.

Modesty in Dress

You have been invited to give a presentation at this convention on the topic of modesty in Islām. Express your feelings and thoughts through poetry.

Moderation in Expenditure

You are a volunteer at a debt help agency. You receive a case of a person who has fallen into a large debt due to their spending habits.

Income: £1000 a month.

Their necessities each month equal £650, however they end up spending £1500.

Draw up a detailed budget plan for them to help them save and repay their debt.

Additionally, provide some advice on the importance of moderation.

Importance of Women in Society

What is the reward of looking after and bringing up a girl? Support your answer with a ḥadīth.

____

____

____

____

Design a colourful poster on the importance of women in society.

Personal Hygiene

Imagine you have a friend who has recently accepted Islām. He has emailed you saying he has heard that Islām places great emphasis on ṭahārah and wants to know more about it.

Write an email response to your friend explaining to him the ādāb of personal hygiene in your own words. Remember this is an informal piece of writing as you are writing to your friend.

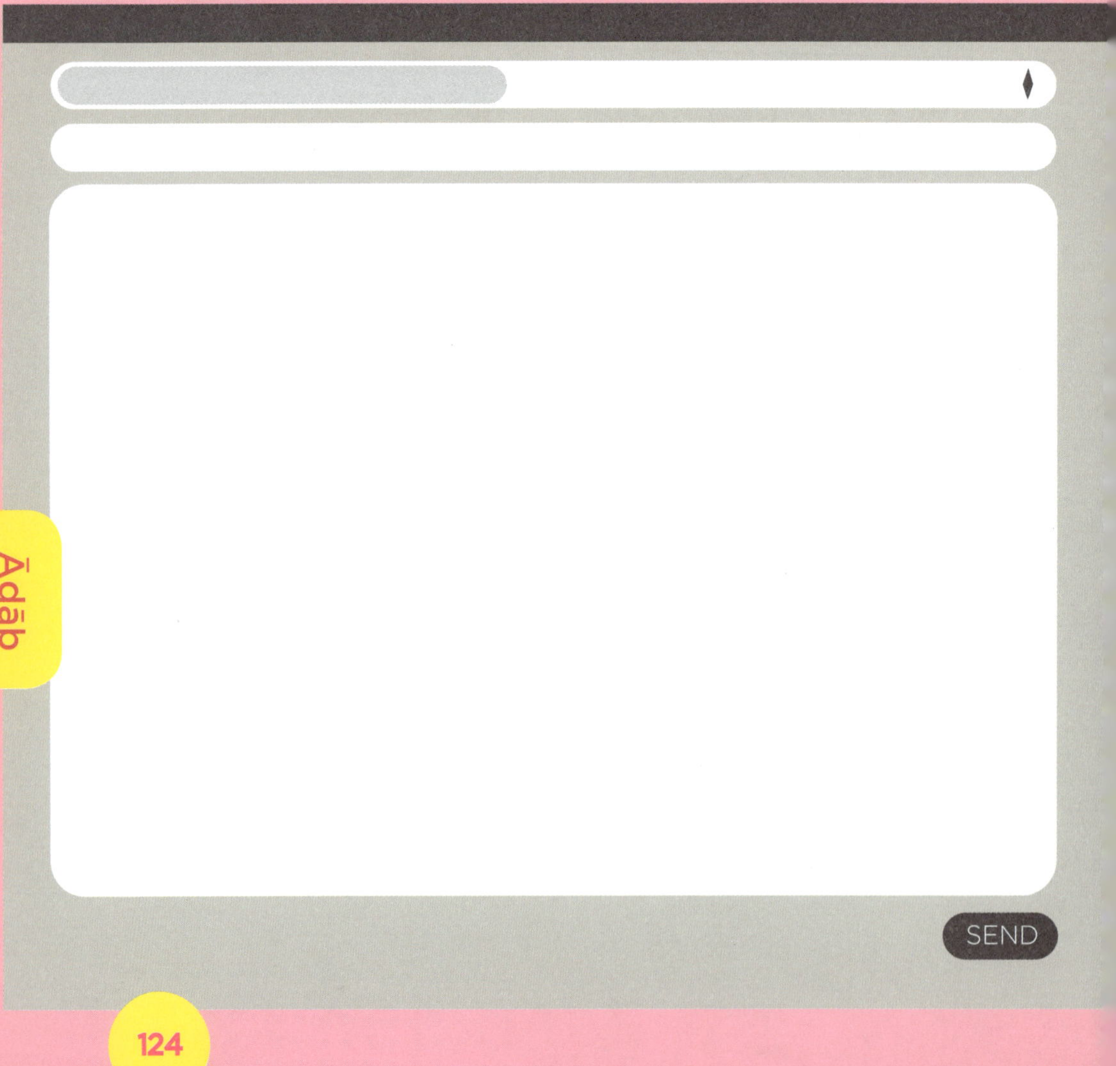